Approximately in
the Key of C

TONY CURTIS
Approximately in the Key of C

2015

Published by Arc Publications
Nanholme Mill, Shaw Wood Road,
Todmorden OL14 6DA, UK
www.arcpublications.co.uk

978 1910435 41 2 (pbk)
978 1910435 42 9 (hbk)
978 1910435 43 6 (ebk)

Cover photograph:
'Currach No. 18' by Liam Blake

Editor for the UK and Ireland:
John W. Clarke

For Madge and Mae –
a lifetime singing
in the key of C

CONTENTS

I have a friend I value here,
And that's a quiet mind.

JOHN CLARE

THE MOLE AND THE COSMOS

for Philip McCracken

I have taken down
a piece
of the night sky,
just for the night.

At mole's suggestion
I've put it by the window
where it looks glorious
against the mountains.

Some say moles are blind,
but it's just that they love
to look at things far away,
                    like stars.

Sometimes when I step out
to look at the night sky
I have to ask mole
what's what, where's where?

And mole, as if he were
a poor country fellow
naming wildflowers,
lists off the constellations:

Southern Cross, Flying Fox,
Bernice's Hair, Winged Horse,
Great Dog, Water Bearer,
Painter's Easel, Chained Maiden.

Mole's deep voice,
sunk like the roots of a tree,
sturdy, reassuring –
you just know he's right.

Michael Egan made a set of uilleann pipes
in 1850. Now they lie silent in a glass display
case at The Museum of Country Life

under a sign that says:
'Approximately in the key of C'.
I love the beauty of those words.

You can't but admire the care and precision
Michael put into making these pipes –
as tuned to this life as possible.

For isn't everything, if looked at closely,
a little off key: lovers and dancers
only a step out, a step away;

talkers on the tips of their tongues;
towns at no distance;
doors and drinkers slightly ajar.

I'd like a copy of that sign to hang on my wall.
Especially in winter, when the poems are buckled, bent,
every one of them *'Approximately in the key of C'.*

FROM THE CENTRAL MENTAL HOSPITAL

I am here again this morning
talking, laughing, singing
with the patients: the lost, the hurt,
the just plain blown-to-bits sad.

A few miles away at Islandbridge
in the War Memorial Gardens,
a garden full of birdsong,
the Queen of England is laying a wreath

for forty-nine thousand five hundred
Irishmen who fell in the Great War,
young men who left the best
of themselves lying in the mud.

Sitting here amongst the patients,
I wonder how many have lost their minds
in No-man's-land? How many are crossing it still?
From this crumbling trench I watch them, pity their step.

THE HUNTER

for Paula Meehan

This morning I called
to where she is wintering out
in a timber hut by the sea's edge.
Everything is grey and leans
away from the wind,
except for the stove pipe
which is straight as a tall tree.
I knocked, but nobody was home:
the teapot was still warm;
the settle bed unmade; a book
lay open on the table: *Captain Ahab
And the Lives of Nantucket Sailors.*
I imagined her further on down the beach,
somewhere beyond the dunes,
reading the waves, the sky, the islands —
hunting that fierce, featherless, solitary
little creature so benignly called a poem.

IN THE WILDERNESS

I met Moses in the asylum,
in a yellow room that smelt of sorrow.

He'd given up the sweeping robes
and carrying a wooden staff.

He was wearing denims
and a T-shirt that said

Follow me on Twitter.
In his small way

he was still leading lost
souls out of the wilderness.

When he stood up, he was
smaller than I had imagined.

Together we read a poem
about Connemara ponies.

Blessed creatures,
he said they were.

He had the deepest
brown eyes.

But it is his voice
I will remember:

it was ten thousand miles
of dusty roads;

it was a parched riverbed,
a dried-out well;

more broken twigs
than biblical thunder.

When I was leaving,
he handed me a scrap of paper

with two lines
written out in pencil:

> *I have a friend I value here,*
> *And that's a quiet mind.*

It was his map
out of the wilderness.

AMHRÁN

i.m. Michael Hartnett 1941-99

Blackcap
Reed Warbler
Meadow Pipit
Thrush
Skylark
Wagtail
Cuckoo
Starling
Goldfinch
Wren
Hartnett
Our
Sweetest
Songbird

THE BLACKBIRD'S LULLABY

Soon the ice will melt,
and the blackbirds sing along the river...
HENRY DAVID THOREAU

Blackbirds are great sleepers.
With their pillow of feathers

and their harvest moon eyes,
they hold the night within.

Only the old know this,
or so an old woman told me.

She may have been out
on the end of a branch, swinging.

No matter.
I left her by the river

with her breadcrumbs
and her knowledge.

But now, every time I think
of blackbirds, I think of her.

And I have been thinking
a lot about blackbirds,

for these nights
I hardly sleep.

You could say I dream
more than I sleep.

Like everyone
I have my worries

but at my age
I don't worry

about my worries.
They are part of me,

my dips and hollows,
my feeble legacy.

I could blame
my poor physical

condition,
my tiring heart,

my tattered soul,
fretful in the dark.

In truth, I think it's
this troublesome trade:

obsessively adding
word to word.

Hammering the dark into light
until the night is almost gone.

Until the page creaks like
a gate almost off its hinges.

I read in a magazine
that the silver light

from a laptop can affect
your circadian rhythm.

Perhaps that's so,
but my rhythm

has always been
off beat. When young,

I was often found asleep
face down in a book;

I could as easily nod off
in the light as in the dark.

My doctor says I should hum
to myself like an old Buddhist:

I am ready for sleep.
I am ready for sleep.

But I am not ready.
I cannot sleep.

I can only close
my eyes and dream.

And what, you ask,
do I dream of?

Sleep, mostly,
pure, forgetful sleep.

That, and one
recurring dream:

I am walking
across a snowy field,

occasionally stopping
to look back

at the long curve
of my footsteps in the snow.

There's nobody else, no one
but me and the white tundra.

In the distance are two trees,
or things that look like trees –

they may well be a broken fence
blown into a heap by the wind.

Occasionally,
there is birdsong.

When I close my eyes
I imagine it's a nesting blackbird

snuggled down –
no, closer than that –

cradled in a thousand peckings
from a summer field: moss,

dried grass, twigs, sheep's wool,
seeds, roots, leaves.

Small things gathered, no,
filched from under blue skies

for the slow release of warmth
on winter nights such as these.

I envy that blackbird
its nesting warmth,

its sheltered sleep,
its black and feathered dreams.

I read in a book
that if left alone

blackbirds
die in their sleep.

Though I've never seen
an old blackbird

I've often beheld a splay
of black feathers beneath a tree.

I suppose in the end
it all comes down to time.

Year upon year,
the weight of hills and hollows

makes everything
creak, even your sleep.

All things must pass.
So perhaps it's simply that:

time.
Not that I worry

too much about time.
Truth is, as each night passes

I know I'll never
be so young again.

Not now, not now,
not now…

UNUSUALLY DUSTY

My computer crashed last night.
It was as if the house burned down,

but no fire brigade arrived,
no ambulance,

no detectives came
to dust for prints,

no priest called to tell me
he was sorry for my troubles.

Just you, standing
in the doorway, asking,

Did you back it up?
And I had to say

I hadn't even indicated,
hadn't even put it into reverse.

Don't say you've lost everything.
You can't have lost the new manuscript.

Well, not exactly: the dusty
scribe who lives inside of me,

that flustering old pedant
who likes the sound of dust settling,

who finds words frayed things
unequal to their task,

he wrote it all down
in his slow doddery way,

word by word,
with pen and ink.

Acoustic, you might say,
before it all went electric.

BLESS

When Emily Dickinson was my age, she was dead –
she had been dead four years.
If I live long enough I'd like to visit her house –
no, her room – in Amherst, Massachusetts.

I've seen a photograph – the honeysuckle tree
by the open window with the lace curtains moving –
beneath it, there's the small square writing table
where, no doubt, her ghost now sits dressed in white.

I would then like to visit the Amherst cemetery. I imagine
there will be a creaking wooden gate, a gravel path –
and, if all is well, her small grave will be covered
in wildflowers – wild – and wilding in the wind.

SNOW-CAPPED

Snow geese fly north a little earlier
and the leaves fall day by day

Old dog, old car, old stories, old friends,
and the fence needs mending yet again.

Old Jacket, old cap, old shoes, old road,
and the door needs painting yet again.

Snow geese fly north a little earlier
and the leaves fall day by day

Old flesh, old bones, old aches, old pains,
and the bath needs filling yet again.

Old lips, old breasts, old sighs, old laughter,
and the bed needs making yet again.

And the far-off snow-capped mountain
looks more beautiful every day

TALKING TO THE WALLPAPER MAN
ABOUT A SCULPTOR

At a tea break in the wallpapering, Kevin looks at 'The Scarecrow's Brain' on the table and the 'Piece of the Night Sky' on the bookshelf. Curious, he asks who made them. I tell him they were made by the sculptor Philip McCracken. "Strange, aren't they?" he says. "What's he like?"

He lives on Guemes island
in a wooden house that looks out
over the islands and the Pacific.

He lives close to nature: you see deer
and chipmunks from his studio door.
In fact, he is very like a heron himself.

*I'm not familiar with herons, says Kevin,
grey or any other colour.*

Then I suppose
you won't know
what I mean.

He can be very like a mole:
there are days he burrows,
digs deep into the earth of himself.

*No, says Kevin, that's no help.
I know nothing about moles.*

Well, let me see now. He's also
very like a barn owl:
sometimes he just watches and listens.

*No, I'm completely lost. Maybe his art
is beyond me, says Kevin.
Would he be any good at wallpapering?*

He'd be brilliant at it. Exceptional.
But he'd have to design all
the paper himself.

And then the hanging of it would
take some time. I imagine he'd hang each
sheet as if he were hanging a painting.

Then he is odd, says Kevin,
like a lot of artistic types.

No, not odd – independent.
He just has to do
things his own way.

Philip can spend days
upon days, hour upon hour,
carving wood and chiselling stone.

Now that I look at them closely,I see the
great craftsmanship in each piece.
I suppose they are valuable.

To him each piece is priceless,
but he leaves his door unlocked.
Besides, no one can steal

what he has. It's buried
too deep inside him.
Like the heron's gaze,

the bear's strength,
the mole's tenacity,
the barn owl's patience.

He sounds like a forest, says Kevin.

Yes, that's it!
That's exactly it –
he is like a forest.

He gathers.
He gives shelter.
He nourishes and shades.

And in the autumn
he turns and changes
and dreams new life.

The way to his heart is marked
with stone paw prints, bronze feathers,
copper leaves, wooden birdsong.

THE FALLEN OAK

i.m. Seamus Heaney 1939 -2013

Early morning, passing through the kitchen,
I catch Eavan's voice on the radio.
She's saying, *Seamus was only seventy-four.*
His passing is shocking. He will be immensely missed.

Momentarily, I think to myself, *Poor Eavan,*
she is losing her mind. But then I feel
the pull of her grief as my world too
stops turning. Through the window

I see green leaves lower their heads,
watch clouds fall away in tears,
blackbirds filling the trees. Then,
almost in plain chant, I hear my soul say,

In the forest of poetry the great oak has fallen.

ELECTRIC LIGHT AND BUTTER LAMPS

Well, Seamus, I was rereading your *Electric Light*.
It's a book I find myself returning to again and again,
but last night was the first time I noticed the poems
were photoset in the Wirral, Birkenhead –
I could hear the cold Irish air blowing in off the Mersey
as patient hands set the poems page by page
working late into the night by electric light.

Then I thought of Mallory and Irving,
two Birkenhead boys who perished
on a great white mountain in Tibet,
where poems are written on prayer flags
and chanted by an old Buddhist by butter lamp.

One evening, reading Seamus's books, I noticed they were all signed
except one, *Electric Light*. I put the book in my bag and carried it around
until I met Seamus. It took some time, so for weeks the book was always to hand. I got to know it intimately; even the publisher's notes
were interesting. *Electric Light* was photoset in Birkenhead, the small
Merseyside town where George Mallory and Sandy Irvine were raised.
On the rainy June night Seamus signed *Electric Light* we spoke about
Birkenhead, Everest and prayer flags; out of that came this small poem
for Seamus & Marie.

The Sliabh Luachra barn lifts her
wooden skirt, dusts herself down,
then dances to reels and jigs.

Her shuffling feet wake
the fox in the field,
the blackbirds in the trees.

Their sudden scatter revives
the drunk floating along in the dark,
heading home. "Play on!" he shouts,

"We have the moon on the run,
and I can see my old father
dancing, cracking the flags.

He loved to see a barn dance,
a moon waltz,
a man raise his glass

to the piper, the fiddler,
the box player and the singer.
Play on, lads!" he shouts, "Play on!"

THE OLD PAINTER'S JOURNEY

In a piano stool that sits
by the back door
I keep, not Schubert's music,
but a pair of old boots
only good enough now for gardening.

The most marvellous pair
of old boots I ever saw
were worn by a seventy-year-old
Lucian Freud in his self-portrait:
'Painter Working. Reflection.'

Naked, he stands like an old chieftain,
the battle lost, no glories to paint,
just the dust and the rage. Although
I imagine, through a child's eyes,
he looks like an old horse left out in the rain.

But as I said, it's the battered old boots I love.
There is only shuffling in them now.
Lucian must have thought them perfect footwear
for an old painter's relentless journey
from his bed to the fierce solitude at his easel.

TWO POEMS

i.m. Elizabeth Bishop 1911-79

1. HOUSE

You wondered how I got the house
in North Haven, Maine.
Well, I saw it in the newspaper.
Wooden, faded cedar,
lonely as my grandmother's house.

I called the number. A woman's voice
asked, "And what do you do?"
In case she didn't trust poets or poetry,
I replied, "I like to paint a bit and watch
the sandpipers running on the wet sand."

"As long as you're neat, and there are
no dogs or men involved, you'll do."
"I'm allergic," I said, "neat as a seamstress."
"You're a poet, aren't you?" she said.
"Come now! The sandpipers are waiting."

35

2. SELF-PORTRAIT NUDE WITH LOTA

If she had been born a boy, she said,
she would have been a rough sailor.
But she was born a girl and grew up
a drunk who drank with disappointed sailors.

If she had been born a bird, she said,
she would have been a shy sandpiper
chasing the waves in and out all day,
not a care in the world but the weight of water.

And yes, if she could have been born an animal,
she said, she would have been the moose
that came out *of the impenetrable wood*,
stood on the country road and stopped her bus.

And if she could have been born a place,
she said, she would have been a sheltered bay
with a fisherman's hut and a red boat bobbing,
or an island with a smouldering volcano at its heart.

But the story goes she lost *Everything*!
Starting with her father, then her mother,
then her mother's mother and her mother's father,
then her mother's sister, then her uncle…

One by one until everyone was gone,
even her lovers, the casual, the precious.
Even the old loved house in Nova Scotia.
Then she herself fell away, poem by poem,
                              she was autumnal.

ૐ

Do you know she painted watercolours?

A tall wooden house in Key West;
the porthole in her cabin; a crumpled hotel room
in Paris, all higgledy-piggledy, the air
thick with cigarette smoke and longing.

Having read her poems and her letters,
having looked at her frail little drawings,
I imagine somewhere there is a watercolour
called, 'Self-portrait Nude with Lota'.

In it Elizabeth is bending over Lota
as she shampoos her lover's long black hair.
Across the valley the forest bush
is darkening and darkening.

It is probably kept in a drawer
out of the Brazilian light.
Occasionally someone looks at it
and wonders who these naked women are.

Or perhaps, now that I think on it
more than likely she burnt it,
her life, like her past,
gone up in flames.

GUNNIE MCCRACKEN

I was born in the make-do hardiness
of the Shetland Islands, always small
for my age, like a Shetland pony.
My father was a fisherman. My mother
a woman who says she fell for his fair
hair, but we know, me and my sisters,
she fell for his touch and went rumble
tumble into his bed. I'm the eldest, Gunnie,
born five months after the wedding.
We've worked it out, me and my sisters.

Did you ever do a handstand at the edge
of a cliff to look at the world upside down?
The sea looks like the sky,
and the sky looks like the sea,
only there are no boats in the sky,
just the weaving, feathery seagull boats.
I've heard my father call seagulls gunnies.
He may have been making a bit of fun
for my sisters, but I loved that he thought
seagulls were small flighty creatures like me.

My grandfather was a fisherman. My grandmother
a woman who fell rumble tumble into his bed.
Our mother, Bonnie, was her eldest,
born five months after the wedding.
We've worked it out, me and my sisters.
They are all small, like gulls. We come from speckled eggs.
Only this morning a neighbour said to me, "Gunnie,
step away from the cliff's edge, the wind might take you."
He could see the bird in me: the feathers in my hair,
my white arms ready to unfold, to stretch out and fly.

EVERYWHERE

*Everywhere I go, I find a poet has
been there before me.*
SIGMUND FREUD

Everyone should have a rhinoceros
and a blackbird on their shelves,
and four clouds hanging on the wall
between Picasso's 'Nude Woman in a Red
Armchair' and Magritte's 'The Son of Man'.

I know I do.

And upstairs where I keep my dreams,
my cactus, my lizard and my camel,
I sleep with a pillow of feathers
under my wings; it helps me dream of flying.

*There are rumours
I was once a bird.*

In the morning, when you walk naked
out of the lake your breasts,
sway in the wind like foxgloves
or in summer light like Carolina jessamine.

*Oh yes, some suggest
I was a gardener,
a leafy herbalist.*

In a glance, I am back in Paris.
It's midnight, and the yellow moon
is shining on the Seine. In the hotel foyer
silver keys jangle on the night porter's belt.

*Perhaps I was a late night
concierge whose life was lit*

by city lights, a nodding
acquaintance of an old tailor.

He looks like Manet getting ready to paint the sunrise.
He holds out a jacket,"Chinese Silk, Indian cotton, Irish tweed.
Finely woven," he says, "made to measure. Fits any condition
from paranoia to schizophrenia, painting to poetry."

Ah yes, that's it,
it is all coming back to me now,
I was a psychoanalyst.

Stitched and mended by the woman
who nightly turned down my bed,
turned down my kisses, my hands,
yet, like the earth, accepted my seed.

Or just maybe
I was a monk.

Blessing the seeds prayer by prayer
until there were no prayers left for what grew.
That must have been when I turned to poetry.
Then sighing helped more than prayer.

I remember it all now, the dark,
and the long deep sighs.

You have to admire the persistence of clouds.
They have been endeavouring for millions of years
to get it right, trying on one shape, then another,
big thick black clouds in the morning,
then changing their minds in the afternoon
and putting on wispy, skimpy little numbers,
practically veils, something that goes with summer blue.
You admire their choice, remove your own clothes
to chance a naked swim or a lie-down on warm earth,
but just as you are about to step into the brightness,
the clouds have changed their minds and slipped
back on some flabby grey overalls. Or sometimes
the clouds simply give up and slouch on the horizon.
You can tell they are depressed by the way they fold
themselves over the hills like a funeral shroud.

Then suddenly one morning like snow geese
they pick themselves up and head north.
There they let their heavy grey backs and shoulders
settle on the islands, the Orkneys, the Shetlands,
softening and softening into white mist, becoming
ghosts. And like ghosts, clouds are not afraid
of being run into, even by a wobbling cyclist
trying to avoid a crazed bumblebee that's lost
its flowers, its pollen, its way in the mist.
And bees are another thing, but we can discuss
them later, when the clouds lift, the sky clears
and the flowers open to the warming sun.

Hannah Barnes was born on a ship out of New Orleans.
Her mother was buried at sea. Her father, Dan, gave
her to the Benedictine nuns in Cobh. She was raised
between their prayers and their silence. All her life
she loved what the sun did to a stained glass window.

Most days, but especially in winter, Hannah would
stand by the sea's edge talking to her mother.
Eventually, following a call, she went to teach
in a convent with the Sisters in Rio. There, she
wrote poems and stories she heard from old sailors.

The American poet, Elizabeth Bishop, loved her work.
She said every word had a claim on its existence, her lines
fell onto the ear as easily as waves onto a shore. Some say
Hemingway began *The Old Man and the Sea* after he read
Hannah's story, *The Blue-eyed Fish*. He said it made him cry.

She was thirty-six when she disappeared. The one
unusual thing about that usual day: it was her birthday,
the thirteenth of April. Sister Mary Immaculata said
Hannah was last seen heading onto the pier at midnight,
running over the stones as if someone were calling to her.

THE OLD GREY HERONS

"What are we now?" you ask.
I want to tell you we are a river,
but in truth we are two birds,
two old grey herons.
So I try to tell you of one
I saw standing by a river
in Oregon: a thin creature
that reminded me of you.
I'm not sure if we like each
other anymore, but the old love,
like the silver in your hair,
will never fade.
Watching that heron
a stillness came over me,
as if my soul had opened
a heavy door;
it was the exact same stillness
I felt the first time I met you.

After a winter of floods, months of thick,
burdensome cloud, the sun has finally
broken through; it is a glorious morning.
The sun on my face is a blessing.
It has me thinking of the Russian poets,
how very cold they were for so very long.
Osip Mandelstam wrote his poems in frost.
I remember poor Marina Tsvetaeva
saying, "Write as if God is watching you."
I have a pen and Chinese notebook to hand
but I feel no gaze upon me, except for one
ragged-feathered seagull. Marina would say
God is watching through that bird's clear eyes.
If it was a white dove, I might believe.

TWO POEMS FOR GARY SNYDER AT EIGHTY-FIVE

1. One Hundred Words on the Old Buddhist

Sometimes when I make a cup of tea,
and sit by the window
looking out across the hills,
I think of Gary Snyder
up on Crater Mountain

drinking tea made from snow-water,
watching out for forest fires.
How old was he –
twenty-two, twenty-three?
I remember reading he spent
days naked in the clouds, where
only eagles had to face his bare cheeks.

The branch tapping on my window
reminds me the old poet, logger,
Buddhist, is eighty-five today.
He climbs a different mountain now,
higher, steeper,
and though the air is thin,
I watch him steadily climb and go on.

2. A Wish in One Hundred Words

I am sitting on the back
of a fallen tree at Samish Bay.
I can't help wishing
the old poet was here.
We could eat oysters
rolled in breadcrumbs,
the way he likes them.
Maybe he'd recite some poems
about the Skagit River,
the full moon over Desolation Peak.

I could show him the slightly tattered
first edition of *The Back Country*
I bought in Portland.
Yes, in Powell's Bookstore.
Signed, I could carry it home to you:
an offering from the mountain trails,
a grain of sand from the Columbia River;
an autumn leaf from the Ish River country.

ASH

i.m. Michael Stanley, died September 11th 2012

Eleven years after the twin towers fell
my mother's brother, Michael, died.
When she phoned to tell me,
I was walking the beach at Skerries,
the tide way out, the harbour empty.
I knew from her voice it was bad news:
I could hear the glass shattering
around her; feel the dust rising;
the bricks fall; the metal bend
as another tower went down.
I imagined her standing by the window,
looking out over the garden,
the grass, the path, the walls
covered in ash, and the ash still falling.

WENDELL

His wife told me she had begun
to fear Wendell's end was near,
but she thought, not yet, that he
had at least another summer in him.

He didn't. He died sitting on
the porch, his last breath unheard.
She found him in the old chair,
his head sunk a little to the side.

She closed his eyes,
then left him sitting there
as if he were about to get up
and head out into the woods.

For he was wearing his cap,
and his dog lay where it always did
in the stillness at his feet,
a stillness that now filled the house.

"Wendell was a talkative man," she said,
"when he got going on a story,
Mother always compared him
to a washing machine on spin cycle.

When I found him gone, finally
at peace, with not another word to say
or add to any story or argument,
it was a kind of heavenly sadness.

So I just added some scented candles
and left him sitting in his old chair.
On the third day I buried him.
Well, I had to. That's the law."

FOR THE LIGHTHOUSE KEEPER'S DAUGHTER

Pledged to three years climbing
the stairs day and night to polish
the light, so the beam can travel
deeper and deeper into the dark.

And what's it like in there? Is it all stillness?
Are there chairs lined up against the wall?
Is there a clock ticking? Is it damp or dusty?

Is there a wood-stove, a row of tall windows?
Do they look out on a city street from childhood
or a meadow with a donkey, a duck and a goat?

Can you see the beach where you
used to walk your black dog?
Do the boats come and go with the tide?

Did they let you bring your memories, your
photographs, your books, or are you all alone,
troubled only by salty ghosts rasping the air?

Is the tower cold like a cell? Is there a grey bed?
Can you hear voices sighing, singing,
laughing, calling from the passing ships?

Should I write? Does the postman visit each day?
Is he burdened? Does he come by bicycle or by boat?
Do you hear him whistling on the rocks below?

Have you etched your name in salt on the window?
Have you written an elegy? Are the lines inscribed
on your heart? Is there a pattern to your day?

Well now, don't worry; I have a plan.
I can see you shaking your head. But wait!
It is a good plan; it's not like the others.

I am baking a pie. I intend to put in a file,
a chisel and a hammer. And in case it is dark,
I am including some candles and matches. Tarot cards.

For company, I am putting in old poetry books
from Sappho to Dante, Shakespeare to Hartnett.
And I'll put in a book on birds, weather and clouds.

I'll include a roll of cloth – blue silk, perhaps –
some small needles, coloured threads and a thimble.
You could use it for drinking nips of tea.

So I'll add some tea leaves, a few smokes,
and squeeze in your old records and the record
player. Where would you be without Bob?

With a day book and a box of pencils,
there will be little room left for your black dog,
but she swears she's invisible and she misses you.

Yes, you're right, it is a big pie.

But I've bribed the guard to look away as I pass.
I want to help; there is so much darkness, and
as far as I can make out, only one solitary lightkeeper.

THE STUBBORN HISTORIAN

He was going back home, he said,
back *to the occupied territories*
north of the Ulster border, though
the border had long vanished into grass.

His people came from farmland in Fermanagh,
somewhere between Lisnaskea and
Enniskillen: a string of crooked fields
close to the quiet, reedy waters of Lough Erne.

After thirty years he still whistled Fenian tunes,
still pointed to where shops were blown to bits.
At every street corner he'd name someone dead,
someone most of us had buried long ago.

Away from his homeland he had kept it all,
shelf upon shelf of wounded memories,
in the cold, grey cell of his occupied soul.
He was a stubborn historian who could not lend
                                    a moment's peace.

EASTER MONDAY 1917

The morning after Christ rose from the dead,
Philip Edward Thomas ascended into heaven
from a field in France. They must have just missed
each other in the lane, shadows, though the mud of Arras
and the mud of Calvary must have been on their boots
and on their hands, when they stepped into the light.

CIVIL WAR

My grandfather knew two men who were
in the Civil War, Jack and William Brown,
brothers, one on each side.

When he spoke of them, he'd say:

Jack had blue eyes.
  Willie had blue eyes.
Jack went to Mass on Sundays.
  Willie went to Mass on Sundays.
Jack married a girl from Dublin.
  Willie married a girl from Belfast.
  And that was the difference:
Jack died for Ireland,
  Willie died for all of Ireland.

Now that my grandfather is dead
I can't ask him where they came from
or in which country graveyard they are buried.

And that's another sadness, for wouldn't
it be a fine thing to lay flowers on their graves
and recall my grandfather's name to them.

What's odd is their dead ghosts haunt me.
Yesterday, during a creative writing class,
a boy asked me "What's an oxymoron, sir?"

I said, "It's where two contradictory words
appear side by side: *act naturally, old news, ill health.*
My own favourites are: *customer care, safe bet, routine surgery.*"

I asked him if he could think of an oxymoron.
"Bad sex," he said, brightening. Then the boy beside him,
his brother, leaned in and shouted "Civil War!"

"That's right," I said, "a perfect example."
And there I stood looking at the smiling brothers,
seeing the ghosts of Jack and Willie.

"Do you know about the Civil War?" I asked.
"Yes, sir, we watched *Lincoln* last night. It was good
but slow; too many words and they never said who won."

"The Irish film was better," his brother said.
"Which one was that?" I asked.
"The Wind that Shakes the Barley, sir.
Cillian Murphy. A lot more killing and cursing.
A lot more action. In America, they had to march
hundreds of miles in uniform to kill each other.

In Ireland, they only had to cross the street
or walk the length of a field or trundle through woods
to shoot each other, to…" He was going to go on

but a girl at the back of the class
crashed into the conversation
"Civil War! I get it now, sir.

Like what goes on at home, the squabbles
with your sisters, your brothers, your father, your mother,
the stuff you don't tell the neighbours about."

"Happy families," the small girl beside her
uttered almost to herself,
but everyone heard, and everyone understood.

THE CURE

"One hospital in Greece had thirty-five gardeners and no gardens."
News, RTÉ 1

I know that hospital,
its whitewashed walls,
its marble floors,
its windows that look
onto narrow dusty streets.

And the patients?
Yes, I know them too.
Farmers mostly, folk from the hills,
men used to terraced olive fields,
women who care for goats and bread.

In the hospital's sterile corridors
and leafless bare wards
these gentle folk found it hard
to heal. Many gave up, or returned
home to die amongst their olive trees.

Some caring soul noticed their loss.
So he brought in thirty-five gardeners
to plant herbs and wild flowers in urns,
window boxes, pots, hanging baskets,
and place them in the wards and halls,

until the wards were a blaze of colour,
the air scented with sweet honey,
sage and olives, and whatever else
a green leaf adds to a room.
In this way they began to heal.

Now when I pass through the wards
or walk the corridors in the morning,

I like to hear the patients
talking leaves and blooms with the gardeners
or laughing at their own disasters.

Yesterday, I heard an old woman
ask what colour Dragon Arum was
and where it got its name.
"Arum," the dusty, unshaven,
blue-shirted gardener said, "*Dracunculus Vulgaris.*

It's red like the spike of a dragon's tail.
Though my father always said
It was more like a young man's prick."
"Ah," the old woman said, "I remember it now,
I grew them in my own wild garden when I was young."

THE LAST BREATH

Sleep now, as under that ancient lamp, all twined together, tired out
with so much talking, so much listening, so much toil and play.

SAMUEL BECKETT

The morning he proposed
I was stirring porridge,
or I may have been about to add some
honey and raisins to my own bowl.
He found honey too sweet,
said the black raisins
pulled at his false teeth.

He saw the raisins in my hand
and was about to complain
when he remembered his proposal.
Romance! I tell you there was more
romance in that small blue bowl –
it had a golden leaf at its heart,
a laurel I think it was.

He put down the newspaper – *Le Monde*,
he'd later laugh at the significance of that –
and stared at me with his sky-blue
eyes; he knew how to unbutton me.
He had masterful hands,
played Schubert up and down my back.
I could feel the notes pulsing through his fingers.

Then he proposed again, but this time
he meant it. He whispered it into my hair,
"Suzanne, will you do me the honour."
He was old-fashioned, like dray horses,
black waistcoats and polished shoes.
The porridge was left on the table while we went at it
in the warmth of our crumpled feather bed.

Years of walking over the Wicklow hills
with his father, of cycling and swimming,
had given him the tightest little derriere,
sweet as honey. We lay for hours in a stillness
so complete we never found it again,
and that was our loss. Still, I loved him
with every breath, down to my last.

After the rumble
    and the tumble,
  the rock and roll,
when the feathers
    and the breath
  have floated softly
back down to earth,
    f abulous to watch
        your breasts swell,
      your stomach stretches
until your bellybutton pops out,
your nipples grow large as saucers,
                dark as chocolate;
                    good enough
            for a small mouth to suck.
    Everything becomes circular:
            your body curves into
            melons and avocados;
        even your voice deepens, goes
                    slightly round.
            For a girl it is all
        moons and autumn leaves.
    For a boy it is bicycle wheels
        and hot air balloons.
            And here's
            the magic,
            the alchemy,
    the miracle of it all:
everything has sides
except a pregnant
        woman.
She is like a bird
    in a cloud,
        its flight,
    its free fall,
    its brightening
    Hallelujah.

Do poets ever reach their destination?
I ask not because I think they are like country buses –
though their minds are often overcrowded,
and they do tend to take the long way round –
I ask because any I've ever met
have been uneasy, watchful,
just arrived or just about to leave,
restless as the postman on his bicycle.

In truth I was thinking of ships,
rusted old cargo ships,
especially those you see late at night
out beyond the bay,
their light fading,
their cargo a mystery,
their destination unknown.
Too late, alas, to wish the captain fair weather.

Last week, at the end of the pier
I hailed a sailor, *Welcome home!*
"Ah no," he said, "we docked last night. We're heading out."
The end of a voyage is the beginning of a voyage.
I wished him fair weather.
As I watched his frail craft batter the wind
I thought, it is the same for poets,
the end of a poem is the beginning of a poem.

And so I ask again,
do poets ever reach their destination?

When I was a child
my grandmother told me
that unlike the sun and moon
the North Star never moves.
So what does it do? I asked.
Well, she said, it hangs
around all night like a poet
drinking in the darkness,
making its own light
for the joy of others,
like you and me.

Tony Curtis was born in Dublin in 1955. He was educated at Essex University and Trinity College Dublin. An award-winning poet, Curtis has published nine warmly received collections. His most recent titles are: *Folk* (Arc Publications, 2011); *Pony*, with drawings and paintings by David Lilburn (Occasional Press, 2013); and *Currach*, with photographs by Liam Blake (2013). His poems were also included in *Days Like These: Three Irish Poets,* along with Paula Meehan and Theo Dorgan (Brooding Heron Press, Waldron Island, Washington Sate, USA, 2009).

In 2003 Curtis was awarded the Varuna House Exchange Fellowship to Australia. He has also been awarded the Irish National Poetry Prize and has read his poetry all over the world to great acclaim. He is a member of Aosdána.

ACKNOWLEDGMENTS

Grateful acknowledgment is due to the editors of the following publications in which some of these poems have appeared: *Agenda* (England); *Clover* (Washington State); *Drawn To The Light: Poems from Poets of the Seventh Skagit River Poetry Festival* (Washington State); *The Clifden Anthology*; *The Stony Thursday Book*; and *What We Found There: Poets Respond to the Treasures of the National Museum of Ireland*.

'The Headland at Skerries, April 8th' was written for *Verbal Sun: Poems in Braille*, edited by Diane Sadler and Philip Coleman. 'In The Wilderness', 'The Mole and the Cosmos' and 'Fair Weather' were filmed and recorded for inclusion in 'The Poetry Archive' which is held at University College Dublin's special collections library.

The author would like to thank Liam Blake, Michael Coady, Theo Dorgan, Sally and Samuel Green, Sean McDowell, Paula Meehan, Pat Mooney, Anne and Philip McCracken, Jerry and Kathy Willins, Mary, Oisin, and all his family. A blessing on them all, and on everyone at Arc Publications.